UNDERSTANDING THE PARANORMAL

INVESTIGATING BIGFOOT, THE LOCH NESS MONSTER, AND OTHER CRYPTIDS

HEATHER MOORE NIVER

Britannica Educational Publishing

IN ASSOCIATION WITH

ROSEN

EDUCATIONAL SERVICES

Published in 2017 by Britannica Educational Publishing (a trademark of Encyclopædia Britannica, Inc.) in association with The Rosen Publishing Group, Inc.
29 East 21st Street, New York, NY 10010

Distributed exclusively by Rosen Publishing.
To see additional Britannica Educational Publishing titles, go to rosenpublishing.com.

First Edition

Britannica Educational Publishing
J.E. Luebering: Executive Director, Core Editorial
Anthony L. Green: Editor, Compton's by Britannica

Rosen Publishing
Jacob R. Steinberg: Editor
Nelson Sá: Art Director
Brian Garvey: Designer
Cindy Reiman: Photography Manager
Karen Huang: Photo Researcher

Library of Congress Cataloging-in-Publication Data

Names: Niver, Heather Moore, author.
Title: Investigating Bigfoot, the Loch Ness Monster, and other cryptids / Heather Moore Niver.
Description: New York : Britannica Educational Publishing, 2017. | Series: Understanding the paranormal | Includes bibliographical references and index.
Identifiers: LCCN 2015045375| ISBN 9781680485721 (library bound : alk. paper) | ISBN 9781680485783 (pbk. : alk. paper) | ISBN 9781680485554 (6-pack : alk. paper)
Subjects: LCSH: Cryptozoology—Juvenile literature. | Sasquatch—Juvenile literature. | Loch Ness monster—Juvenile literature.
Classification: LCC QL89 .N67 2016 | DDC 001.944—dc23
LC record available at http://lccn.loc.gov/2015045375

Manufactured in the United States of America

Photo credits: Cover, p. 1 Victor Habbick/Shutterstock.com; p. 5 Science Source; p. 7 © Topham/The Image Works; p. 9 Private Collection/Archives Charmet/Bridgeman Images; p. 11 Popperfoto/Getty Images; p. 12 Ernst Haas/Getty Images; p. 14 © ZUMA Press, Inc./Alamy Stock Photo; p. 17 Photos.com/Thinkstock; p. 19 © Ivy Close Images/Alamy Stock Photo; p. 20 © Shawn McCullars; p. 22 Chuang Zhao; p. 24 © Lebrecht Music and Arts Photo Library/Alamy Stock Photo; p. 27 Internet Sacred Text Archive (www.sacred-texts .com); p. 28 Fox Photos/Hulton Archive/Getty Images; p. 30 Keystone/Hulton Archive/Getty Images; p. 32 Private Collection/ © Look and Learn/Bridgeman Images; p. 35 Private Collection/Bridgeman Images; p. 36 Rijksmuseum Kroller-Muller, Otterlo, Netherlands/Bridgeman Images; p. 37 Alinari/Art Resource, NY; p. 39 Tengku Bahar/AFP/Getty Images; p. 40 © AF archive/Alamy Stock Photo; interior pages backgrounds © iStockphoto.com/Kivilvim Pinar, © iStockphoto.com/mitja2.

CONTENTS

INTRODUCTION

People have always been interested in animals. Early in the history of civilization, hunters tracked down and domesticated the animals of their own surroundings. These remote peoples also listened eagerly to travelers from far places who told of strange beasts they had seen and even stranger ones they had only heard about.

Because early writers lacked scientific knowledge, they often confused fact with hearsay. Several books of travel and natural history that were dated from pre-Christian times and the Middle Ages were widely read, and their reports of fantastic animals were accepted. New versions, even more bizarre, were handed down. In the 1st century CE, the Roman scholar Pliny the Elder published a 37-volume *Natural History*, which was a massive compilation of 2,000 earlier works, and in it described many legendary beings, including hybrid creatures with the heads of dogs and bodies of people.

The most famous travel book of the Middle Ages was *The Voyage and Travels of Sir John Mandeville, Knight*, written in the mid-14th century. The mysterious writer's fanciful descriptions of monsters were probably derived from the writings of other noted authors.

The legendary manticore, as depicted in a Latin bestiary (an animal-based story), had a human head, lion's body, and dragon's or scorpion's tail.

In 1544 Sebastian Münster wrote the popular *Cosmographia Universalis*, which had vivid descriptions of dragons and basilisks. Even the great Swiss naturalist Conrad Gesner, in *Historia Animalium* (1551–87), described the unicorn and winged dragons.

CHAPTER ONE

THE BIGFOOT FAMILY

With many alleged visual sightings but no verified evidence to date, Bigfoot remains a fascinating story to follow. Bigfoot stories go back hundreds of years, to native people who told tales of an apelike animal roving through the forests.

APELIKE APPEARANCE

Most descriptions of Bigfoot and his purported relatives are fairly similar to one another. He is said to be a big furry animal. Sasquatch, for example, is variably described as a primate ranging from 6 to 15 feet (2 to 4.5 meters) tall, standing erect on two feet, often giving off a foul smell, and either moving silently or emitting a high-pitched cry. Footprints have measured up to 24 inches (60 cm) in length and 8 inches (20 cm) in width. A Soviet scientist, Boris Porshnev,

This depiction of Bigfoot from the 1967 film created by Roger Patterson was said by some to be authentic, but others deemed it only a human wearing a costume.

suggested that Bigfoot-like creatures could be remnants of Neanderthals, but most scientists do not recognize the creature's existence.

CHASING CRYPTIDS

A cryptid is an animal that cannot be scientifically identified. But just because an animal is called a cryptid doesn't mean it isn't real. At one time the giant squid, the kangaroo, and the mountain gorilla were all considered cryptids. Could the likes of Bigfoot also be proven? It's the work of cryptozoologists, or those who study these mythical monsters, to come up with the hard facts that prove—or disprove—the existence of some of the world's most elusive beasts. Some cryptozoologists get right out there in the wild to search for the unknown. Cryptozoology is not generally considered an official branch of science.

ALL IN THE FAMILY: BIGFOOT, SASQUATCH, YETI, AND OTHER "RELATIVES"

The bipedal beast goes by many names, depending on where in the world it is spotted. Sasquatch (from Salish *se'sxac*: "wild men") is called by many names, including Bigfoot. It is said to be a large, hairy, humanlike creature believed by some people to exist in the northwestern United States and western Canada. In Louisiana a similar creature called the four-toed Honey Island Swamp Monster allegedly prowls the swamps, and in Florida a "skunk ape," known for its foul stench, reportedly roams the Everglades.

Bigfoot-type creatures seem to be spotted all over the world. The Abominable Snowman is known as the Ycti or "magical crcaturc" in Tibct and the Nee-gued in the state of Sikkim in northeast India. The Siberian counterpart of Bigfoot and the Abominable Snowman is called

This drawing of a Yeti, also known as the Abominable Snowman, shows a creature that was said to roam Tibet and other mountainous regions.

the Almas. The Almas seems to more closely resemble an extremely hairy human being, with skin sometimes visible through its long red fur. In India the Mande Burung, or "forest man," is known for its black and gray fur and towering above its other bipedal relatives at 10 feet (3 meters) tall. England's Devonshire Devil dates back to some mysterious footprints in the snow in 1855. These prints are unique among Bigfoot stories in that they seem to be part hoof. In China the Yaren supposedly creeps through the mountains of the Hubei Province. Chinese myths have included enormous ape-like beings and wild men, but the Yaren stories started around the 1970s.

THE SCIENCE OF SASQUATCH

Investigations of reported Bigfoot-like creatures have been impeded by a great many hoaxes and pranks. One notable false story took place in 2008 when the "evidence" touted by two men in Georgia who claimed to have discovered a Bigfoot carcass turned out to be nothing more than fake fur and rubber feet. Still, some scientists are on the case to come up with an explanation for the Bigfoot stories.

British explorer David Thompson is sometimes credited with the first discovery (in 1811) of a set of Sasquatch footprints, and hundreds of alleged prints have been presented since then. Visual sightings and even supposed photographs and filmings (notably by Roger Patterson at Bluff Creek, California, in 1967) have also contributed to the legend, though none of the purported evidence has been verified.

An expedition to Mount Everest returned with photographs that were alleged to show the fresh footprints of an Abominable Snowman through the snow.

In 1960 *National Geographic* magazine reported that famed explorer Sir Edmund Hillary, together with Desmond Doig, returned from an expedition in Nepal triumphantly brandishing what some considered an authentic Yeti scalp. Hillary refused to confirm whether or not he believed it had once adorned the head of a Yeti. After further examination, scientists determined that the fur was from a goat-like animal found in Nepal known as a serow.

Over the years, other investigations of the furry beast usually reveal the evidence to be something far more common, such as bear tracks. In some cases, such as India's

Mande Burung, traces of the beast might be evidence of a gigantic ape called *Gigantopithecus*, which lived around 200,000 years ago.

In 2012, Oxford University's geneticist Bryan Sykes studied samples of hair said to be from the Yeti, Bigfoot, and Sasquatch. He spent a year testing samples of DNA from all over the world. Sykes said that his results showed that two of the samples were matches for a polar bear's jawbone that was found in Norway's Arctic region in

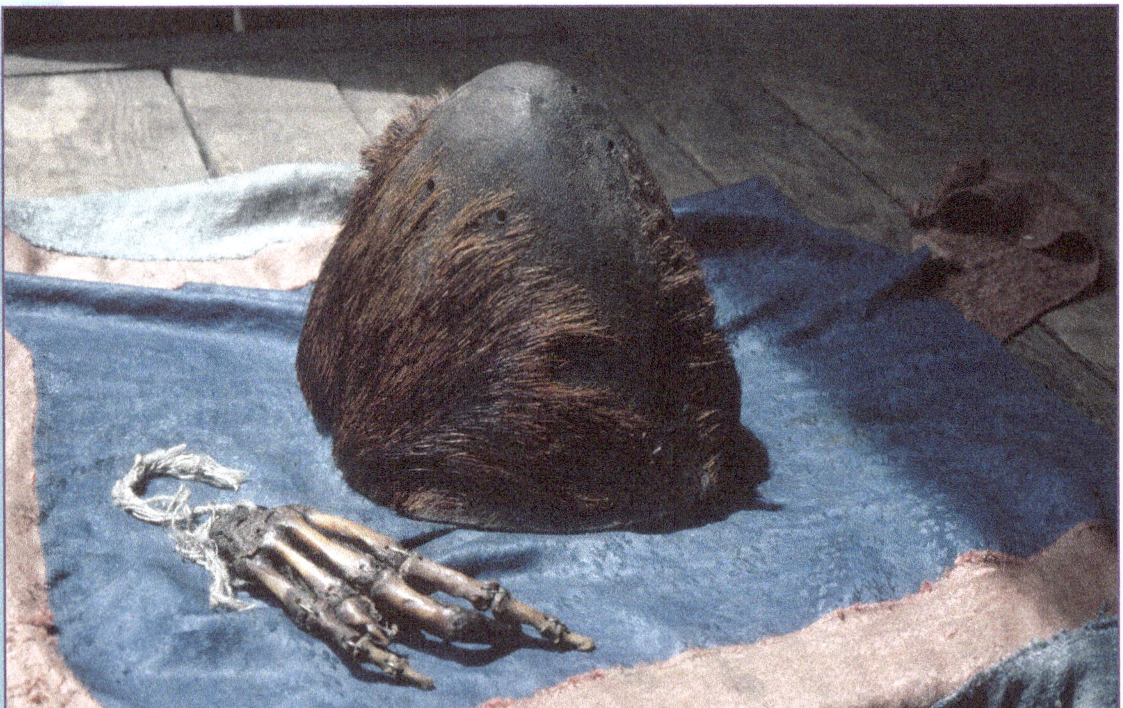

The Khumjung monastery near Mount Everest displays what they claim to be a Yeti's skull and hand.

2004. That bone might be 120,000 years old! Many scientists are waiting for Sykes's work to be critically evaluated before they come to any conclusions.

Among the ranks of believers is primatologist and leading chimpanzee expert Jane Goodall. In a November 2006 interview she told National Public Radio, "Well now you will be amazed when I tell you that I'm sure that they exist." Still, she later admitted in an October 2012 interview with the *Huffington Post*, "Of course, it's strange that there has never been a single authentic hide or hair of the Bigfoot."

Actor Peter Mayhew played the Bigfoot-reminiscent Chewbacca in the massively popular *Star Wars* film series. Widespread belief in the big furry beast is prevalent enough that, while in costume on set in the Pacific Northwest, Mayhew had to stay close to crewmembers who wore bright-colored vests. No one wanted to risk Mayhew being shot if he was mistaken for Bigfoot!

THE FUR IN FILMS AND FICTION

With such a rich history of myths and legends about Bigfoot, it should be no surprise that movies, fiction, and popular culture have embraced him. *Harry and the Hendersons* (1987) offers audiences a charming character, while the Abominable Snowman makes an appearance

The 1987 film Harry and the Hendersons *is just one cinematic presentation of the infamous Bigfoot as a friendly, charming beast.*

in *Monsters, Inc.* (2001) as an unfairly banished beast who wishes others saw him as "adorable" rather than "abominable." The classic holiday television special *Rudolph, the Red-Nosed Reindeer* (1964) depicts a gruff but misunderstood Abominable Snowman.

The possibility of Bigfoot's existence is explored in TV network Animal Planet's *Finding Bigfoot* series. On this recurring show, the hosts, somc of whom arc scientists, travel to follow up on reported sightings of Bigfoot. Some of the *Finding Bigfoot* hosts were once or are currently members of the Bigfoot Field Researchers Organization (BFRO), an organization founded in 1995 to investigate the existence of Bigfoot.

CHAPTER TWO

FLIGHTS OF FANCY: DRAGONS

Of all the monsters in myth and folklore, the dragon is the most familiar and the most feared. Winged dragons with flames and smoke pouring from their nostrils dominate the legends of many countries. The various species whose parts were combined into the dragon's hybrid form differed from one land to another.

HISTORY AND LORE

According to a legend of the Middle Ages there once lived in a distant pagan land a dreadful monster called a dragon. The flapping of its great batlike wings could be heard for miles around. From its nostrils came clouds

Many stories from the Middle Ages tell of Saint George slaying a dragon.

of smoke and flames that brought death to those who breathed it.

Every year a young girl was offered to it to prevent the dragon from rushing upon the city and destroying all the inhabitants. One year the lot fell to Princess Sabra, daughter of the king. She was saved by the valiant St. George, youngest and bravest of the seven champions of Christendom.

ROC

In Arabic legends, the roc (or rukh) was a gigantic bird with two horns on its head and four humps on its back that was said to be able to carry off elephants and other large beasts for food. It is mentioned in the famous collection of Arabic tales, *The Thousand and One Nights*, and by the Venetian explorer Marco Polo, who referred to it in describing Madagascar and other islands off the coast of Eastern Africa. According to Marco Polo, Kublai Khan inquired in those parts about the roc and was brought what was claimed to be a roc's feather, which may really have been a palm frond. Sinbad the Sailor also told of seeing its egg, which was "50 paces in circumference."

Various evidence has been collected over the years that indicates that very large bird species once actually existed. Consider the elephant bird (a member of the genus *Aepyornis*). These giant flightless birds stood 10 feet (3 meters) tall and lived on the island of Madagascar, becoming extinct

Arabic legends depict the roc as an enormous horned bird with a humped back that is so large that it is able to fly off clutching an elephant.

sometime in the last 1,000 years. The eggs of the largest species of elephant birds were apparently the largest eggs ever laid by any animal, measuring as much as 35 inches (89 centimeters) in circumference. *Aepyornis* may have given rise to the legend of the roc.

With his magic sword, Ascalon, he wounded the monster so badly that the princess was able to put her sash about its head and lead it to the marketplace of the town. There St. George slew it with one blow. Won over to the Christian faith by this deed of their champion, the people were baptized.

This is but one of the many dragon stories told in the lore of different countries. Before the time of Columbus and the Age of Discovery, sailors refused

This detail of a dragon from the Nine Dragon Wall of the Forbidden City of Beijing, China, offers one image of the fierce dragon.

to venture into unknown seas for fear of encountering dragons and other monsters of the deep. Old maps show the uncharted seas filled with strange creatures having wings, horns, and claws of such enormous size that they could crush a ship. The dragons of Chinese and Japanese myth and art were reptiles with batlike wings and claws and were supposed to spread disease and death among the people. For ages the dragon was the emblem of the former imperial house of China.

FIERY FACTS

Superstitions about dragons may have been based on the fact that mammoth reptiles roamed the prehistoric world. Dinosaurs lived in the ages before man appeared on Earth. However, there may have been some reptiles of great size at the time of the primitive cavemen of Europe. Such beasts would easily give rise to legends of monsters such as the dragons.

In July 2015, researchers in northeastern China discovered archaeological remains of *Zhenyuanlong suni*, a large feathered cousin of the velociraptor. It became the largest winged and feathered dinosaur species discovered to date. Tellingly, the Chinese word for "dinosaur" is *konglong*, or "terrifying dragon." Unlike dragons of legend, however, researchers are certain that *Zhenyuanlong suni* was flightless.

This illustration was prepared by an artist working with the archaeological team that discovered the fossils of Zhenyuanlong suni, *a large dragon-like dinosaur, in northeastern China in 2015.*

In the East Indies certain small lizards, 7 or 8 inches long, are known as dragons. They are about the color of tree bark. The skin along their sides between their legs spreads out into a kind of parachute, enabling them to fly among the branches of the trees in which they live. There are about 20 species, all harmless.

DRAGONS IN FILM AND FICTION

Dragons have filled volumes over the years. J. R. R. Tolkien published *The Hobbit; or, There and Back Again* (1937), which introduced readers to a fantastic world whose inhabitants—elves, dwarfs, wizards, and the furry-footed hobbit Bilbo Baggins—fight and win against an evil dragon named Smaug. Tolkien's Smaug was brought to life in the 2013 film adaptation *The Hobbit: The Desolation of Smaug*. Lewis Carroll wrote a still-memorable poem about the vicious dragon known as the Jabberwocky in *Through the Looking-Glass* (1871). Again this dragon is quite vividly brought to film, as in Tim Burton's quirky *Alice in Wonderland* (2010), in which it is voiced by Christopher Lee. The list of dragons in fiction goes on and on, including Michael Ende's *The Neverending Story* (1979; adapted to film in 1984), *Between Planets* (1951) by Robert A. Heinlein, and George R. R. Martin's A Song of Ice and Fire series.

British author J. K. Rowling captured the imagination of children and adults alike with her best-selling series of books about Harry Potter, a young sorcerer in training. Brimming with myth and magic, the Harry Potter series (both fiction and films) included drag-

Lewis Carroll's stories of Alice feature a poem about the fearsome dragon known as the Jabberwocky in Through the Looking-Glass ***(1871).***

ons as well as many other cryptids. Just one example is found in *Harry Potter and the Chamber of Secrets* (1998) when Harry and his fellow champions must face some vicious dragons. Rowling also penned the companion book—also fictitious—*Fantastic Beasts and Where to Find Them* (2001), which includes details about dragons and other creatures.

U.S. author Christopher Paolini wrote the Inheritance cycle, a four-book collection of fantasy stories that feature a dragon named Saphira. The series, aimed at young adults, includes *Eragon, Eldest, Brisingr,* and *Inheritance*. These books tell a classic story of a hero on a quest while delving into themes such as good versus evil, loyalty, honor, and friendship. *Eragon*, a movie based on the book, was released in 2006.

CHAPTER THREE

SCALY SECRETS: THE LOCH NESS MONSTER

Legends about sea serpents (marine animals that resemble gigantic snakes) date back to ancient times. Although tales of sea serpents have continued to exist throughout the centuries, no animal has been captured so far that has not proved to belong to a previously well-known group.

Sea serpents often bear similarities to dragons. The Leviathan, a sea serpent from Jewish mythology, is mentioned several times in the Hebrew Bible as a many-headed, gliding, coiling monster of the sea. In Greek mythology, the Hydra was a gigantic monster with multiple heads. For each head that was cut off, the monster grew two new ones. There is a real-life sea creature called a hydra that appears to have multiple heads and can regrow parts of its body, but it is only about 1.2 inches (3 centimeters) long.

This 16th-century woodcut shows a sea serpent attacking a ship.

Other real-life sea monsters include the oarfish and giant squid. The oarfish, a tropical creature that usually lives in deep water, is a ribbon-shaped fish that can grow to a length of about 30.5 feet (9 meters) and a weight of 660 pounds (300 kilograms). Giant squids, sometimes found in the waters of Scandinavia, Denmark, the British Isles, and the eastern coasts of North America may grow to 50 feet (15 meters) and look like a serpent when swimming on the surface.

THE LOCH NESS MONSTER

Loch Ness is a lake lying in the Highland council area of Scotland. With a depth of 788 feet (240 meters) and a length of about 23 miles (36 km), Loch Ness has the largest volume of fresh water in Great Britain. Like some other very deep lochs in Scotland and Scandinavia, Loch Ness is said to be inhabited by an aquatic monster. Many sightings of the so-called Loch Ness Monster have been reported, and the possibility of its

Scotland's Loch Ness is rumored to be the home of the elusive Loch Ness Monster, a creature that has graced stories for centuries but eluded scientists.

existence—perhaps in the form of a solitary survivor of the long-extinct plesiosaurs—continues to intrigue many.

The first written account of Scotland's secretive serpent was in a biography of the 6th-century Irish abbot St. Columba, composed about a century after his death. However, it was in 1933 that more serious interest in the creature emerged. On May 2, 1933, the *Inverness Courier* published a report that a local Scottish couple had spotted the famous monster. This report and several more that followed later that year added some splash to the more modern myths. In July of that year, a London couple claimed to have spotted the "dragon" crossing on land. London's *Daily Mail* offered a reward for the Loch Ness Monster's capture. Tales spread like wildfire and were published in newspapers both in England and abroad.

THE SCIENCE OF THE SCOTTISH SCALES

Hoaxes seem to follow almost all modern cryptid stories, and the Loch Ness Monster, or "Nessie," is no exception. In 1934 Nessie's tracks were allegedly spotted, but when plaster casts were sent to the British Natural History Museum, tests showed that they were from a hippopotamus—and a stuffed one at that! A 1934 photograph also gave cryptozoologists hope that the Loch Ness Monster was a real surviving plesiosaur. However, the cold waters

Evidence of the Loch Ness Monster has been hard to come by, but a few photographs, such as this one, are enough for some believers to prove Nessie exists.

of Loch Ness would not support a cold-blooded dinosaur. Furthermore, in 1994 the famous photo was revealed to be a hoax.

Sonar of the lake in the 1960s never showed any solid evidence of Nessie, either. In 1975 sonar and underwater photography were used in tandem and revealed a photograph that plesiosaur supporters hoped would prove their case. Further use of sonar has produced inconclusive readings. In 2008, a television documentary for the series

Monster Quest called "Death at Loch Ness" posed the idea that Nessie's corpse was at the bottom of the lake. As usual, this theory has its supporters and its deniers.

One theory debunking sightings of the Loch Ness Monster swimming just beneath the surface concerns waves known as seiches. A seiche is a kind of wave that may occur in large lakes and in such semi-enclosed bodies of water as bays and sounds. In Loch Ness, they are caused by cold river water flowing into the warmer waters of the loch. Some scientists believe the illusion of a living

CHAMP AND OGOPOGO

Back across the pond, quiet Lake Champlain holds its own scaly mysteries. "Champ" is known as America's Loch Ness. Using hydrophone equipment, researchers in 2014 detected echolocation in different areas of the lake, revealing sounds that some feel could come from none other than Champ.

In Canada a sea serpent called Ogopogo has long been rumored to lurk in British Columbia's Lake Okanagan. The purported monster was captured on film in 1968. The National Geographic Channel TV show *Is It Real?* in 2005 found that this footage most likely showed an ordinary animal such as a beaver or lake sturgeon making a big splash.

creature moving underwater is the result of observers spotting seiches in Loch Ness.

THE LOCH NESS MONSTER IN POPULAR CULTURE

The earliest literary appearance of a sea serpent in Loch Ness is in St. Adamnan's 7th-century biography of St. Columba. Columba is said to have spotted a monster attacking a man in the waters of Loch Ness. Columba then invoked the name of God and drove the beast back.

Literary references to the Loch Ness Monster began in the 7th-century biography of St. Columba, in which it is claimed St. Columba saw a huge monster attack a man in the waters of Loch Ness.

Constance Whyte's *More Than a Legend* (1957) is a compilation of accounts of Nessie sightings. Nessie has also been portrayed often in movies, such as *Loch Ness* (1996), in which a zoologist (played by Ted Danson) seeks scientific proof of the monster's existence, and the comedic cartoon *Scooby-Doo and the Loch Ness Monster* (2004).

Still wondering about the viability of a Scottish sea serpent? Google Street View offers those who are curious about cryptids the opportunity to search Loch Ness to try and spot the elusive Nessie.

CHAPTER FOUR

MARINE MYSTERIES: MERMAIDS

A mermaid is a fabled marine creature with the head and upper body of a woman and the tail of a fish. A male mermaid is called a merman.

BEWARE THE BASILISK

The basilisk was a serpent so horrible that it killed with a glance. Pliny the Elder described it simply as a snake with a small golden crown. By the Middle Ages it had the head of a cock or sometimes a human head. It was born of a spherical egg, laid during the days of Sirius, the Dog Star, by a 7-year-old cock. The egg was then hatched by a serpent or toad. The sight of a basilisk was so dreadful that if the creature saw its own reflection in a mirror, it supposedly died of fright. The only way to kill it, then, was to hold a mirror before it and avoid looking at it directly. The basilisk appears frequently in literature, including in J. K. Rowling's *Harry Potter and the Chamber of Secrets.*

Hans Christian Andersen's fairy tales, including* The Little Mermaid, *feature stories and illustrations of part-human, part-fish creatures called mermaids.

UNDERWATER TALES

Tales of mermaids have been around for centuries. Ancient Mesopotamian mythology includes similar divine or semidivine beings such as the Chaldean sea gods Ea and Oannes. Ea was commonly represented as a half-goat, half-fish creature, while Oannes had the form of a fish but with the head of a man under his fish's head and the feet of a man under his fish's tail. In European folklore, mermaids (sometimes called sirens) and mermen were natural beings who, like fairies, had magical and prophetic powers. They loved music and often sang. Though very long-lived, they were mortal and had no souls.

Irish legend says that mermaids were pagan women banished from Earth by St. Patrick. Ancient tales in the Far East

French artist Odilon Redon's 1910 oil painting Oannes *shows the Chaldean sea god who had a man's head and a fish's body.*

tell of mermaids marrying dragons of the sea. They were in charge of bringing messages from their husbands to human emperors. In Australia, aboriginals know mermaids as yawkyawks, which might be a reference to their hypnotic singing. Similarly, sirens are sea nymphs whose singing was said to have lured men to certain death.

Many folktales record marriages between mermaids (who might assume human form) and men. In most, the man steals the mermaid's cap or belt, her comb or mirror. While the objects are hidden, she lives with him; if she finds them, she returns at once to the sea. In some variants the marriage lasts while certain agreed-upon conditions are fulfilled, and it ends when the conditions are broken.

Though sometimes kindly, mermaids and mermen were usually dangerous to humans. Their

An ancient Greek statue of a Siren dates to the 4th century BCE. It was a tomb statue from a cemetery in Athens.

gifts brought misfortune, and the beings caused floods or other disasters if they were offended. To see one on a voyage was an omen of shipwreck. Mermaids and mermen sometimes lured mortals to their deaths by drowning or enticed young people to live with them underwater.

ARE MERMAIDS REAL?

While there is no scientific evidence for the existence of an aquatic humanoid species, some researchers consider aquatic mammals that suckle their young in human fashion above water—such as the dugong and manatee—to be the origin of mermaid legends. Sailors throughout the ages might have seen these animals from a distance and believed that they were mermaids.

In the late 19th and early 20th centuries, there were occasional news reports of mermaid sightings in the Pacific Northwest. Even as late as the 1960s, the *Daily Colonist* newspaper in Victoria, British Columbia, published a report and alleged photograph of a mermaid spotted by an American tourist on the rocks of Mayne Island. The photograph shows a woman with long blonde hair covering her chest and what appears to be the tail of a porpoise, a seal, or a whale. First published on June 13, 1967, three subsequent reports were published later that month. No substantial evidence was ever produced to corroborate the existence of the mermaid. In 2015 the newspaper's editor-in-chief, Dave Obee, shared the opinion that the photograph was a hoax.

In 2009, the Israeli coastal city of Kiryat Yam became the center of international reports after residents reported sightings of a mermaid living off the coast. Several reports claimed to spot the young mermaid briefly emerging from the waves before diving back under the surface. The town's local council offered a one-million-dollar prize to anybody who could prove the mermaid's existence. In 2013 a video clip purporting to show the mermaid on camera went viral. The clip is blurry, and its so-called evidence

In July 2006, a museum on the outskirts of Kuala Lumpur, Malaysia, featured the supposed remains of a mermaid.

is inconclusive.

To date, no definitive and widely accepted proof of a mermaid has been found anywhere.

MERMAIDS IN FICTION AND FILM

Mermaids, mermen, and sirens swim through well-known

In 1989 Disney made Hans Christian Anderson's tale The Little Mermaid *into a wildly popular animated movie with music.*

literature, such as Lydia Millet's *Mermaids in Paradise* and Hans Christian Anderson's *The Little Mermaid* (which was also made into an animated movie), and movies including *Peter Pan, Hook, Pirates of the Caribbean: On Stranger Tides,* and *Splash*. A mermaid even graces the logo of popular coffee brand Starbucks. Sirens also sing in Homer's *The Odyssey*, and their song echoes in another era via Ethan and Joel Coen's Homer homage movie *O Brother, Where Art Thou?*

But in 2012 mermaids were the talk of the town for another reason. The television channel Animal Planet aired what appeared to be a documentary proving the existence of mermaids called *Mermaids: The Body Found*. The show seemed to include interviews with scientists, but a minuscule disclaimer at the end of the credits revealed that the so-called scientists were actually actors. Most people missed that detail and came away with the idea that the show was factual. In fact, there was so much confusion over the matter that the U.S. National Oceanic and Atmospheric Administration had to issue an official statement: "No evidence of aquatic humanoids has ever been found." Even so, *Mermaids: The Body Found* was so popular that Animal Planet produced a sequel in 2013 called *Mermaids: The New Evidence*.

GLOSSARY

BASILISK In stories and legends, a reptile that can kill people by breathing on them or looking at them.

BIPED A two-footed animal.

CHIMERA A fire-breathing female monster in Greek mythology with a lion's head, a goat's body, and a serpent's tail.

CIVET CAT A long-bodied, short-legged African mammal that is related to the mongoose.

CRYPTOZOOLOGY The study of and search for legendary animals.

DEBUNKING Exposing the falseness of.

DNA Any of various nucleic acids that are located especially in cell nuclei, are usually the chemical basis of heredity, and are composed of two nucleotide chains held together by hydrogen bonds in a pattern resembling a flexible, twisted ladder.

ECHOLOCATION A physiological process for locating distant or invisible objects by means of sound waves reflected back to the sender (such as a porpoise).

FABLE A short fictitious story; especially one intended to teach a lesson and in which animals speak and act like human beings.

GENETICIST A person who specializes in the branch of biology that deals with the inherited traits and variation of organisms.

HOAX An act intended to trick or deceive, or something false passed off or accepted as genuine.

KRAKEN A sea monster of Scandinavian legend.

LOCH A lake, or an arm of the sea especially when it is nearly surrounded by land.

NEANDERTHAL A primate mammal that belongs to the same family as human beings, lived from about 30,000 to 200,000 years ago, is known from skeletal remains in Europe, northern Africa, and western Asia, and is characterized especially by a stocky, muscular build and prominent brow-ridge—called also Neanderthal man.

PLESIOSAUR Any of a group of large Mesozoic marine reptiles with flattened bodies and limbs shaped like paddles.

PRIMATOLOGIST One who studies primates and especially primates other than human beings.

PROPHETIC Of or relating to foretelling of the future.

SALISH A group of American Indian peoples of British Columbia and the northwestern United States;

also, the family of languages spoken by the Salish peoples.

SCAT The feces deposited by an animal.

SEICHE The rhythmic movement of water in a lake or a partially enclosed coastal inlet, such as a bay, gulf, or harbor. Seiches may be induced by local changes in atmospheric pressure. They also may be initiated by the motions of earthquakes and by tsunamis.

SEROW Any of several goatlike mammals of eastern Asia that are usually rather dark and heavily built and some of which have distinct manes.

SIREN One of a group of womanlike creatures in Greek mythology that lured mariners to destruction by their singing.

SONAR A device for detecting the presence and location of submerged objects (as submarines) by sound waves.

FOR FURTHER READING

Anderson, Jennifer Joline. *Bigfoot and Yeti* (Creatures of Legend). Minneapolis, MN: Core Library (ABDO), 2014.

Colson, Mary. *Bigfoot and the Yeti.* Los Angeles, CA: Ignite Publishing, 2013.

Hand, Carol. *The Existence of Sasquatch and Yeti.* Minneapolis, MN: Essential Library (ABDO), 2012.

Hile, Lori. *The Loch Ness Monster* (Solving Mysteries With Science). Chicago, IL: Capstone Raintree, 2013.

Hile, Lori. *Mermaids* (Solving Mysteries With Science). Chicago, IL: Capstone Raintree, 2013.

Nagle, Jeanne. *Investigating the Abominable Snowman and Other Legendary Beasts.* New York, NY: Rosen Publishing, 2012.

Regan, Lisa, and McNab, Chris. *Urban Myths and Legendary Creatures.* New York, NY: Gareth Stevens Publishing, 2011.

Stevens, Robert. *Dragons!* New York, NY: Rosen Publishing, 2012.

Stevens, Robert. *The Loch Ness Monster!* New York, NY: Rosen Publishing, 2012.

WEBSITES

Because of the changing nature of Internet links, Rosen Publishing has developed an online list of websites related to the subject of this book. This site is updated regularly. Please use this link to access this list:

http://www.rosenlinks.com/UTP/crypt

INDEX

Westward Expansion

AMERICA'S PUSH TO THE PACIFIC

THE ERIE CANAL

JEANNE NAGLE

Britannica Educational Publishing

IN ASSOCIATION WITH

ROSEN

EDUCATIONAL SERVICES

Published in 2018 by Britannica Educational Publishing (a trademark of Encyclopædia Britannica, Inc.) in association with The Rosen Publishing Group, Inc.
29 East 21st Street, New York, NY 10010

Distributed exclusively by Rosen Publishing.
To see additional Britannica Educational Publishing titles, go to rosenpublishing.com.

First Edition

Britannica Educational Publishing
J.E. Luebering: Executive Director, Core Editorial
Andrea R. Field: Managing Editor, Compton's by Britannica

Rosen Publishing
Heather Moore Niver: Editor
Nelson Sá: Art Director
Tahara Anderson: Designer
Cindy Reiman: Photography Manager
Heather Moore Niver: Photo Researcher

Library of Congress Cataloging-in-Publication Data

Names: Nagle, Jeanne, author.
Title: The Erie Canal / Jeanne Nagle.
Description: New York : Britannica Educational Publishing, in Association with Rosen Educational Services, 2018. | Series: Westward expansion: America's push to the Pacific | Includes bibliographical references and index. | Audience: Grades 5–8.
Identifiers: LCCN 2017014856| ISBN 9781680487879 (library bound) | ISBN 9781680487862 (pbk.) | ISBN 9781538300121 (6 pack)
Subjects: LCSH: Erie Canal (N.Y.)—History—Juvenile literature.
Classification: LCC HE396.E6 N364 2018 | DDC 386/.4809747—dc23
LC record available at https://lccn.loc.gov/2017014856

Manufactured in the United States of America

Photo credits: Cover, p. 25 Bettmann/Getty Images; p. 5 Encyclopædia Britannica, Inc.; p. 8 Culture Club/Hulton Archives/Getty Images; p. 10 From The New York Public Library/510d47da-2264-a3d9-e040-e00a18064a99; p. 13 Universal Images Group/Getty Images; p. 14 Hulton Archive/Archive Photos/Getty Images; p. 15 Smith Collection/Gado/Archive Photos/Getty Images; p. 17 From The New York Public Library/510d47e1-4d74-a3d9-e040-e00a18064a99; p. 20 Private Collection/© Look and Learn/Bridgeman Images; p. 21 Daniel Borzynski/Alamy Stock Photo; p. 22 Hulton Archive/Getty Images; pp. 23, 30–31 Historical/Corbis Historical/Getty Images; p. 27 Underwood Archives/Archive Photos/Getty Images; p. 29 SuperStock/Getty Images; p. 32 The New York Historical Society/Archive Photos/Getty Images; pp. 34–35 The New York Historical Society/Hulton Fine Art Collection/Getty Images; p. 36 nsf/Alamy Stock Photo; p. 37 Chicago History Museum/Archive Photos/Getty Images; p. 40 Fotosearch/Archive Photos/Getty Images; p. 41 George Ostertag/Alamy Stock Photo; cover and interior pages (banner) Library of Congress Prints and Photographs Division.

CONTENTS

INTRODUCTION

The American frontier was an escape and a place of hope for those willing and able to take their futures into their own hands. Celebrated then and ever since in poetry, short stories, novels, drama, films, music, and paintings, the epic westward movement in the United States has never failed to excite the imaginations of people everywhere.

In the United States, the frontier moved in stages, beginning with the eastern settlements, the original thirteen colonies. After the American Revolution, the pioneers gradually crossed the Appalachian Mountains and went into the Ohio and Mississippi river valleys.

Some settlers arrived with eyes open and were happy with what they found. Many did not expect the real frontier, which was a hard place to live in. Most of the normal expectations of life were missing. One made do with what was available, and normally that was very little. Grinding poverty was the living standard, at least until the frontier began to give way to civilization.

As the country expanded westward, settlers in western New York, Pennsylvania, and Ohio were faced with the problem of transporting goods. The places to sell their farm products were the large eastern cities, such as New York City. In turn, the settlers needed the supplies and manufactured goods that were sold in these cities. Wagon freight was too expensive—it cost a hundred dollars to send one ton of freight from Buffalo to New York City, and the trip took twenty days. The new flat-bottomed river steamships offered cheap transportation, but there were no through water routes between the large population centers of the East and the farmlands of the developing West.

Canals, built to link natural waterways, were the solution. The Erie Canal was the first canal in the United States to connect the Great Lakes with the Atlantic Ocean.

Map of the Erie Canal.

The 363-mile (584-kilometer) canal was constructed from 1817 to 1825 along the Mohawk River, between the Hudson River and Lake Erie. It connected Lake Erie at the city of Buffalo in the western part of the state with Albany, the state capital located in the east. At Albany, the canal met with the Hudson River, which runs south to New York City and empties into New York Bay at the southern tip of Manhattan Island.

The success of the Erie Canal propelled New York City into becoming a major commercial center and encouraged canal construction throughout the United States. With ready access to markets, settlers moved into upstate New York and western territories.

The importance of the canal to the early expansion of the United States cannot be overstated. It opened the Great Lakes region to industry and farming, and it provided a market for manufactured goods from the East. By creating the nation's first east–west water-trade link, the canal encouraged westward expansion.

CHAPTER ONE

WESTWARD HO!

In the middle of the 1700s, both Britain and France controlled land in North America. Britain controlled the thirteen colonies that later became the United States. Under French rule was the area called New France. It included large parts of what is now eastern Canada and also covered much of the Great Lakes region and areas west of the Appalachian Mountains.

Both countries wanted the upper Ohio River valley, in what is now northeastern Ohio and western Pennsylvania. The French built a chain of forts from the St. Lawrence River to the Mississippi and were trading with the Native Americans in the area. However, this land was claimed by Virginia under its "sea-to-sea" grant from England. People from the British colonies were starting settlements in what they called the western frontier.

The conflict over the Ohio River valley led to an epic struggle between the two countries—the French

Map detailing land that constituted "New France," denoted in green, circa the early eighteenth century. The French were at odds with the British over disputed trade routes in the area.

and Indian War, which lasted from 1754 to 1763. By 1760 the British had captured all of New France. The war ended when Britain and France signed the Treaty of Paris on February 10, 1763.

After the American Revolution ended in 1783, this wilderness area became part of the United States of America. The Ordinance of 1787 provided that from three to five states could be carved from the territory's limits. After the land was surveyed, it was quickly occupied. The new country was expanding westward.

OPENING TRADE

Settling the western frontier was one thing. Making it a viable place to live, however, was another. Using what is known as subsistence farming, settlers in Ohio and farther west could certainly feed themselves from their own livestock and whatever crops they produced. Yet farmers and other tradesmen also needed a healthy market for what they grew, raised, or produced. Likewise, western settlers needed to purchase clothes, furniture, and other manufactured goods that came out of eastern cities.

Distance and a certain degree of isolation from the larger, established eastern cities and towns made trade difficult, to say the least. Hauling goods and people by land to what was known then as "the interior" of the United States took quite a while. The shortest distance between two points is a straight line, but there was no straight-through path from the East to the interior, thanks to the Appalachian mountain range. Getting around the Appalachians added time to the journey.

New York City, Philadelphia, and Baltimore were all rivals for the trade of the growing interior of the United States, namely the Ohio River valley and the western frontier. Location favored New York in the struggle. It could tap the lowest route through the Appalachians by way of the Mohawk River valley.

HARNESSING THE MOHAWK

Beginning in the 1780s, various plans were proposed to improve navigation on the Mohawk River. In 1792 the Western Inland Lock Navigation Company was

Print showing travelers on a bridged road that crossed the Mohawk River. The Mohawk was the site of early canal construction in the United States.

incorporated by the state of New York and given the rights to improve navigation on rivers and lakes west of Albany. Under the leadership of Philip Schuyler, the company focused most of its activity on the Mohawk River, clearing the riverbed and digging several short canals to bypass river rapids. Although the company achieved some success in making improvements to the river, it never had the financial resources to tackle the larger navigation obstacles in the river.

The Western Inland Lock Navigation Company, which found itself short of funds and snarled in state partisan politics, never completed its plans. Nonetheless, the Mohawk River still provided a valuable path from the Atlantic Ocean to the Great Lakes, and plans for a new canal were debated. In 1820 the state purchased the company's works, closing the books on the eighteenth-century canal plans. Meanwhile, a new canal project had been gaining momentum in New York State.

SELECTING THE ROUTE

As early as 1808, Albert Gallatin, then secretary of the treasury, made a survey of all available transportation routes in the United States. As a result of this survey, he recommended the building of a great many canals. One of the canals he proposed was

General, President, Canal Builder

Canals were a great help in developing transportation and commerce in the United States. Revolutionary War hero and future United States president George Washington was among the first statesmen to realize how important they might be. He headed the Potomac Company, which was formed to improve navigation along Virginia's Potomac River. The company's plan was to build a trench, with a system of locks, alongside the river's length—in other words, to construct a canal.

The Chesapeake and Ohio Canal, as the project became known, was not completed until 1850. However, several shorter canals connecting rivers were built in the early days of the United States. The first was dug at South Hadley, Massachusetts, between 1792 and 1796.

meant to link the Hudson River in New York with the Great Lakes in the western territory.

The proposed canals were much longer than any that had previously been dug in the United States. In addition, the costs and the engineering problems were so great that most people regarded Gallatin's proposals as impractical. DeWitt Clinton, then the powerful mayor of New York City, thought otherwise. Although originally he had supported a Hudson–Great Lakes link